# Phillis Wheatley

**Emily R. Smith, M. A. Ed.**

# Table of Contents

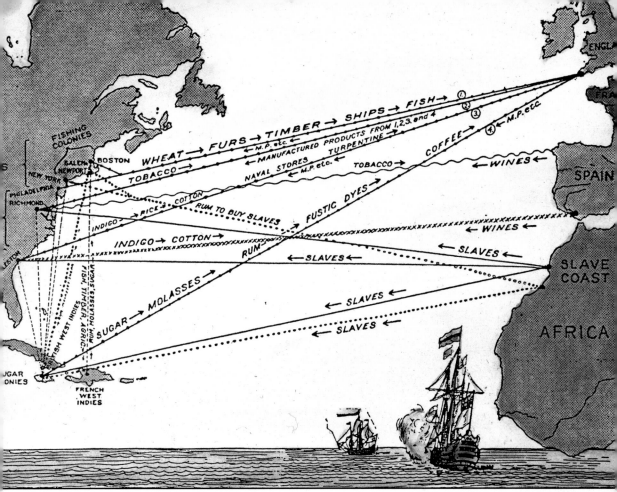

▲ Slave trade routes across the Atlantic Ocean

# An Amazing Journey

Phillis Wheatley was born in western Africa around 1753. When Phillis was seven years old, she was kidnapped. She was taken on a boat to Boston, Massachusetts. Then, she was sold as a **slave**.

Phillis was a very smart little girl. She learned to read and write English quickly. She soon became colonial America's first black poet.

# Learning to Read and Write

A wealthy Boston man bought Phillis. His name was John Wheatley. He wanted Phillis to be a servant for his wife, Susannah. John and Susannah named Phillis after the slave ship that brought her to the colonies. Her last name became Wheatley because they owned her.

Timothy Fitch

Slaves being ▶
brought to
the colonies

## The Slave Ship *Phillis*

A man named Timothy Fitch was a **slave merchant**. That meant that he owned a ship that brought slaves to the colonies. In Boston, he worked with a **slave trader**. The slave trader sold slaves.

▲ This is Boston Harbor where slaves like Phillis were brought on ships from Africa.

The Wheatleys had two grown children. Their names were Mary and Nathaniel. Mary taught Phillis to read and write. Educating slaves was **illegal** (ill-LEE-guhl) in the southern colonies. In Boston, it was not against the law to teach a slave. That doesn't mean that people agreed with doing this. But, the Wheatleys could tell that Phillis was special.

Phillis enjoyed studying. The Bible was one of her favorite books. She learned to write by copying parts of the Bible. The people of Boston often saw Phillis writing on fences or the ground. She would write with charcoal or sticks. Every new subject was exciting for Phillis.

# Slavery in the South

▲ **Map of Africa**

Most slaves were taken from their homes in Africa. They didn't speak English. They were put on overcrowded ships. Those ships spent weeks crossing the Atlantic Ocean. Can you imagine how scared these **captives** were?

The ships took the prisoners to the colonies. Most of them were brought to the big southern colonies. The large **plantations** (plan-TAY-shuns) needed a lot of workers. There were no plantations in the northern and middle colonies. So, there were fewer slaves there.

In the South, there were laws that controlled the slaves. They were called the "black codes." The law against teaching slaves was an example of a black code. Another example relates to church. Blacks were not allowed to go to the same churches as whites. These laws made the lives of black people very hard.

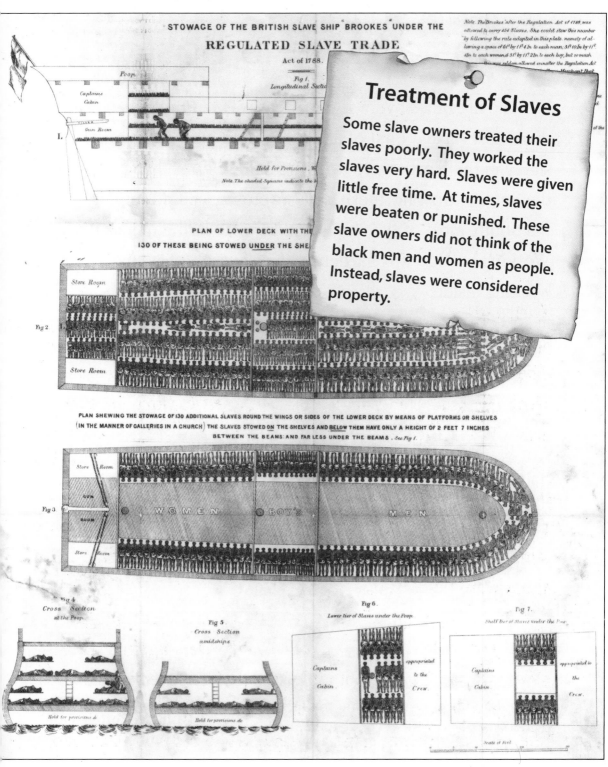

STOWAGE OF THE BRITISH SLAVE SHIP "BROOKES" UNDER THE

## REGULATED SLAVE TRADE

Act of 1788.

Poop.

Captains Cabin

Gun Room

Fig 1.
Longitudinal Section

Hold for Provisions

Note. The shaded Squares indicate the

PLAN OF LOWER DECK WITH THE

130 OF THESE BEING STOWED UNDER THE SHE

Store Room

Store Room

Fig 2

PLAN SHEWING THE STOWAGE OF 130 ADDITIONAL SLAVES ROUND THE WINGS OR SIDES OF THE LOWER DECK BY MEANS OF PLATFORMS OR SHELVES (IN THE MANNER OF GALLERIES IN A CHURCH) THE SLAVES STOWED ON THE SHELVES AND BELOW THEM HAVE ONLY A HEIGHT OF 2 FEET 7 INCHES BETWEEN THE BEAMS: AND FAR LESS UNDER THE BEAMS. See Fig 1.

Store Room

Store Room

Fig 3

WOMEN    BOYS    MEN

Fig 4
Cross Section
at the Poop.

Fig 5.
Cross Section
amidships

Fig 6.
Lower tier of Slaves under the Poop

Fig 7.
Shelf tier of Slaves under the Poop

Captains
Cabin

appropriated
to the
Crew.

Captains
Cabin

appropriated to
the
Crew.

Hold for provisions &c

Hold for provisions &c

## Treatment of Slaves

Some slave owners treated their slaves poorly. They worked the slaves very hard. Slaves were given little free time. At times, slaves were beaten or punished. These slave owners did not think of the black men and women as people. Instead, slaves were considered property.

▲ Diagram of how slaves were packed on the ships

# Life as a Slave in Boston

The life of a slave was never easy. But, Phillis was luckier than most slaves. First of all, she lived in New England. The slaves in the North were usually treated better than slaves in the South. Most northern slaves were household servants. In the South, most of the slaves had to work in the fields all day. Working outside was harder on the slaves' bodies than working inside.

### Kindness?

It's true that the Wheatleys treated Phillis kindly. They even helped her publish her book of poems. However, keep in mind that they did not free her from slavery until 1773. That means she was a slave in their house for 12 years.

▲ Field hands at work picking cotton in the South

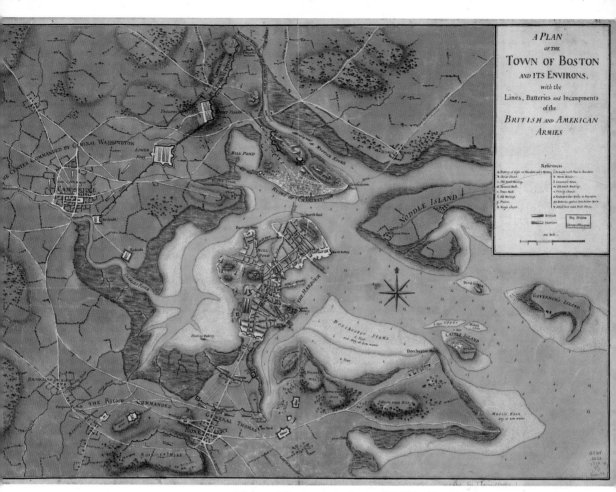

▲ Map of Boston, where Phillis lived

The Wheatleys were kind to Phillis. They knew that she was special and helped her to learn. Phillis once wrote that Mrs. Wheatley treated her "more like a child than her servant." Most slave owners did not treat their slaves like family.

In New England, slaves were allowed to go to white people's churches. But, they had to sit in separate areas. There were not as many laws in the North to control how people treated their slaves.

# Poetry and Religion

Phillis was 14 when her first poem was published. She used poetry like a diary. She wrote about how she was feeling and what she was thinking. This was unusual for colonial poets. Most colonial poets did not share a lot of emotions in their poems.

Religion was important to the Wheatley family. The Great Awakening (uh-WAY-kuh-ning) happened in the 1730s and 1740s. This was a time when **ministers** (MIN-uh-stirs) tried to get more people to join their churches. Ministers traveled from town to town holding outdoor meetings. At these meetings, the ministers helped people get excited about religion.

## Poetry Role Model

Phillis Wheatley was the first black poet to be published. That means that she did not have the chance to study poems by other black people. Instead, she learned by reading poems from Europeans (yur-uh-PEE-uhns). Her favorite poet was Alexander Pope.

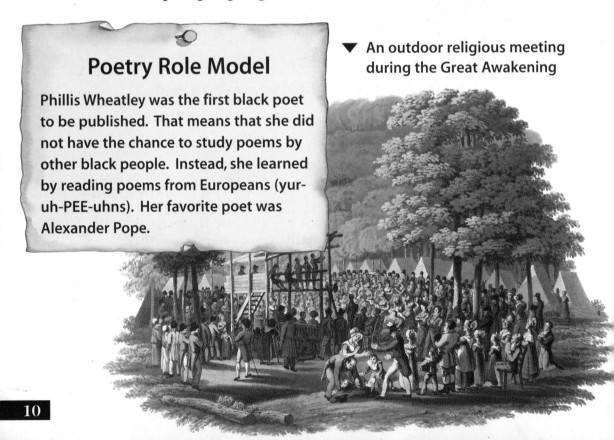

▼ An outdoor religious meeting during the Great Awakening

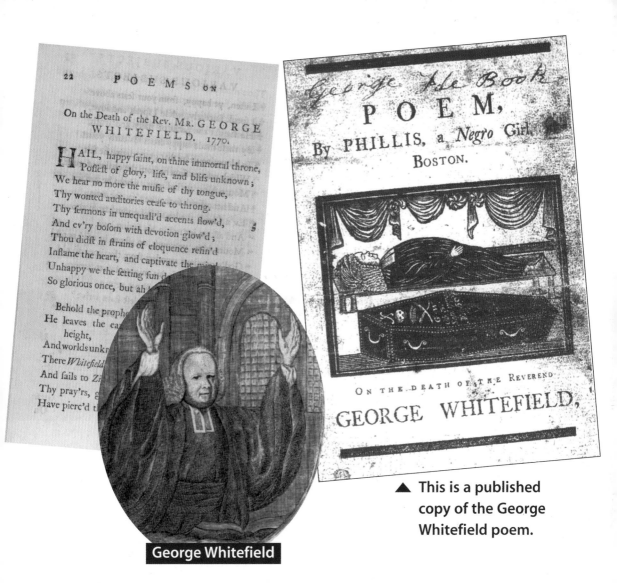

**George Whitefield**

▲ This is a published copy of the George Whitefield poem.

    One minister that Phillis listened to at her church was George Whitefield. He was one of the most famous ministers from the Great Awakening. He was a great speaker. She enjoyed going to listen to Whitefield speak on Sundays. When he died, Phillis wrote a poem about him. The poem was published in Massachusetts and England. This poem made her famous. She was 17 years old.

▲ **King Street in Boston near the Wheatley's home**

# Writing About the Times

The Wheatley family lived in a large house. The house was on King Street in Boston, Massachusetts. This street was right in the middle of the city. There was always a lot going on around Phillis.

This was a difficult time for the people who lived in the colonies. The rulers in England kept passing laws. These laws took freedoms away from the colonists. People felt that this was unfair. Many colonists wanted **independence** from England and the king.

Men called **Patriots** (PAY-tree-uhts) started to **protest** the king's actions. The Patriots were based in Boston near Phillis.

Phillis wrote poems about the events in her city. One poem was about an ex-slave named Crispus Attucks. He was shot during the Boston Massacre (MAS-uh-kuhr). Phillis also wrote about British troops who moved into Boston.

VARIOUS SUBJECTS.   27

On the Death of a young Gentleman.

WHO taught thee conflict with the pow'rs
    of night,
vanquish Satan in the fields of fight?
So strung thy feeble arms with might unknown,
How great thy conquest, and how bright thy
    crown!
War with each princedom, throne, and pow'r
    is o'er,                                       5
The scene is ended to return no more.
Could my muse thy seat on high behold,
How deckt with laurel, how enrich'd with gold!
Could she hear what praise thine harp em-
    ploys,
How sweet thine anthems, how divine thy joys!  10
What heav'nly grandeur should exalt her strain!
What holy raptures in her numbers reign!
To sooth the troubles of the mind to peace,
To still the tumult of life's tossing seas,
                                              To
    D 2

28      POEMS on

To ease the anguish of the parents heart,      15
What shall my sympathizing verse impart?
Where is the balm to heal so deep a wound?
Where shall a sov'reign remedy be found?
Look, gracious Spirit, from thine heav'nly bow'r,
And thy full joys into their bosoms pour;      20
The raging tempest of their grief control,
And spread the dawn of glory through the soul,
To eye the path the saint departed trod,
And trace him to the bosom of his God.

## Christopher Snider

An 11-year-old boy was killed right near Phillis's home. He was shot during an argument on a street corner. The man who shot him was loyal to the king of England. The Patriots were very upset about the death of this young boy. Phillis wrote a poem about him. She agreed with the Patriots and wrote about how terrible the event was.

▲ Published copy of the Christopher Snider poem

▲ Slaves serving dinner
to a wealthy family

# Society Rules

Mrs. Wheatley enjoyed going to social events. Sometimes, she brought Phillis with her. Phillis was invited to read her poetry aloud. This was one way that Mrs. Wheatley made Phillis more popular in Boston.

However, Phillis was usually uncomfortable once she finished her poetry readings. The society women would all sit together to have tea.  Most of the time, Phillis chose to sit at a separate table.  She did not feel welcome to sit with the white women.

One day, Phillis went with Mrs. Wheatley to a friend's home.  When she arrived, Phillis was introduced to Mrs. Fitch.  Mrs. Fitch's husband owned a ship called *Phillis*.  It turned out that he was the man who had brought Phillis to Boston!  Everyone was a bit uncomfortable that afternoon.

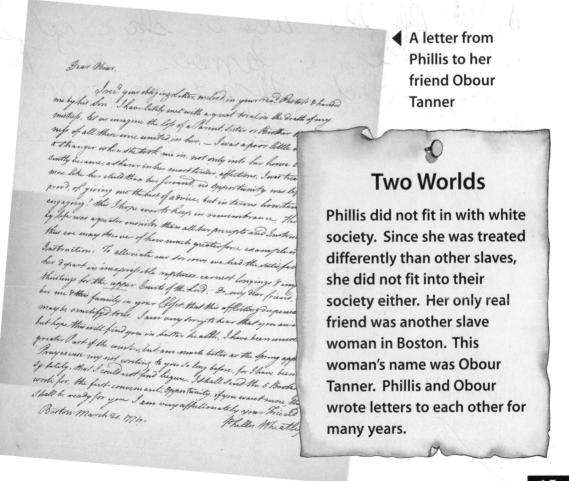

◀ A letter from Phillis to her friend Obour Tanner

## Two Worlds

Phillis did not fit in with white society.  Since she was treated differently than other slaves, she did not fit into their society either. Her only real friend was another slave woman in Boston. This woman's name was Obour Tanner. Phillis and Obour wrote letters to each other for many years.

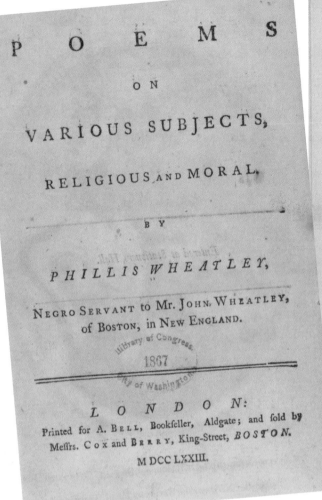

POEMS

ON

VARIOUS SUBJECTS,

RELIGIOUS AND MORAL.

BY

PHILLIS WHEATLEY,

NEGRO SERVANT to Mr. JOHN WHEATLEY,
of BOSTON, in NEW ENGLAND.

1867

LONDON:

Printed for A. BELL, Bookseller, Aldgate; and sold by
Messrs. COX and BERRY, King-Street, BOSTON.

MDCCLXXIII.

The following is a Copy of a LETTER sent by Author's Master to the Publisher.

PHILLIS was brought from *Africa* to *Amer* in the Year 1761, between Seven and Ei Years of Age. Without any Assistance from Sch Education, and by only what she was taught in Family, she, in sixteen Months Time from her rival, attained the English Language, to which was an utter Stranger before, to such a Degree to read any, the most difficult Parts of the Sac Writings, to the great Astonishment of all heard her.

As to her WRITING, her own Curiosity led to it; and this she learnt in so short a Time, tha the Year 1765, she wrote a Letter to the I Mr. OCCOM, the *Indian* Minister, while in *Engl*

She has a great Inclination to learn the L Tongue, and has made some Progress in it. T Relation is given by her Master who bought and with whom she now lives.

JOHN WHEATL

*Boston*, Nov. 14, 1772.

▲ **The first two pages of Phillis's book**

# Poems on Various Subjects

By 1772, Susannah Wheatley thought that someone should publish a book of Phillis's poems. The poems that had been printed in newspapers were very popular. People enjoyed reading Phillis's work in the colonies and England.

It was hard for Phillis to get her work published because she was a slave. Mrs. Wheatley tried to find a colonial publisher. It was very expensive to print books at that time. No one wanted to risk losing money on a slave's book.

So, Mrs. Wheatley found someone in England to print the book. At first, the printer did not want to publish the book. He did not believe that a slave could have written so beautifully. Some important men from Boston told him that Phillis was a gifted poet. After that, the publisher agreed to print the book.

▲ Colonial printing press

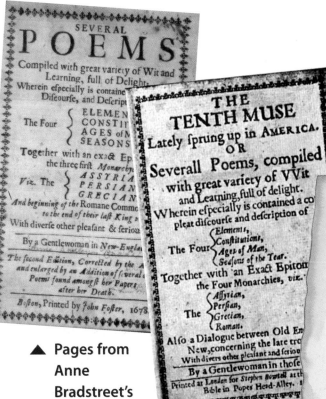

▲ Pages from Anne Bradstreet's book of poems

## Black Woman Poet

Phillis's book was the first book published by an American black person. She was only the second American woman to have a book published. Anne Bradstreet was the first. In 1650, Bradstreet published a book of poems.

# Traveling to England

In May 1773, Nathaniel Wheatley took Phillis to England. She was supposed to meet the Countess of Huntingdon. The **countess** was helping to pay for the publication of Phillis's book.

Phillis enjoyed her visit to England. She got to meet many people who had read her poetry. She was treated better in England than she was in the colonies. Finally, the countess sent an invitation to Phillis. She invited Phillis and Nathaniel to come to her country house.

Unfortunately, Phillis received some bad news. Mrs. Wheatley was very sick. She wrote and told Phillis to come home. Phillis never got to meet the countess. She had to leave England before her book was published.

**◄ A painting of Phillis Wheatley created after she died**

## Book Dedications

Phillis dedicated her book to the Countess of Huntingdon. In those days, a **dedication** (ded-uh-KAY-shuhn) of a book was very important. A book could be popular just because of whom it was dedicated to. The countess decided that the book should have Phillis's picture on the first page. That image is the only known picture of Phillis created during her lifetime.

The dedication page ▼ from Phillis's book

DEDICATION.

To the Right Honourable the

COUNTESS OF HUNTINGDON,

THE FOLLOWING

P O E M S

Are most respectfully

Inscribed,

By her much obliged,

Very humble,

And devoted Servant,

*Phillis Wheatley.*

◀ The picture from the front of Phillis's book

**Countess of Huntingdon**

19

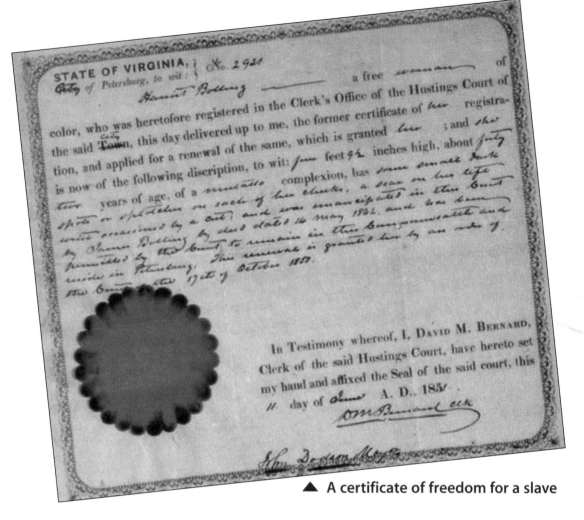

▲ A certificate of freedom for a slave

# Freedom at Last!

In 1773, Mr. Wheatley freed Phillis. She was no longer a slave. But, she continued to live with the Wheatleys. Mrs. Wheatley was very ill and Phillis helped take care of her.

Slaves could be freed in a couple of different ways. Their owners could give them their freedom. This is what Mr. Wheatley did for Phillis. Slaves could also earn money and buy their own freedom. This was very difficult.

▼ General George Washington

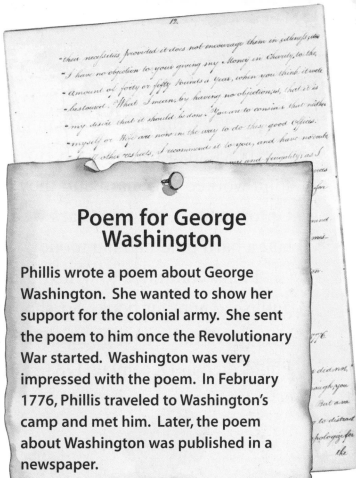

## Poem for George Washington

Phillis wrote a poem about George Washington. She wanted to show her support for the colonial army. She sent the poem to him once the Revolutionary War started. Washington was very impressed with the poem. In February 1776, Phillis traveled to Washington's camp and met him. Later, the poem about Washington was published in a newspaper.

In March 1774, Susannah Wheatley died. Losing Mrs. Wheatley was difficult for Phillis. Phillis had grown close to Mrs. Wheatley over the years.

Phillis had to earn money now that she was not a slave. She decided to try to sell her book in the colonies. The publisher in England sent her 300 copies. She placed advertisements (ad-ver-TIZE-muhnts) in newspapers. The books sold quickly.

Then, the American Revolution started. Ships from England could not bring her books to the colonies anymore.

# "Liberty and Peace"

In 1778, Phillis met a man named John Peters. He was a free black man who lived in Boston. Soon, they were married. John worked very hard and they had a nice house. Unfortunately, the war years were hard. John lost his job and had a hard time making money.

Phillis continued to write during this time. But, she never published another book. So, she was not making much money either. All three of John and Phillis's children died young. Phillis died in December 1784. She was only 31 years old.

## Wheatley's Will

When Mr. Wheatley died in 1778, he was still a very rich man. His will did not mention Phillis. He left no money or property to her. She had been his servant for 12 years. Even though they had treated her like family, was she really family?

◀ Illustration showing a slave in chains

A poem called "Liberty and Peace" was the last one Phillis wrote. During her life in America, Phillis had seen a lot of violence. By 1784, the country had finished a war. People were working together to build a new nation. This poem describes the **patriotism** (PAY-tree-uh-tiz-uhm) felt throughout the states. As always, Phillis wrote with great emotion. Her words tell about an exciting time in the country's history. People today are lucky to have Phillis's poems about the past.

Liberty and Peace—

Perish that Thirst of boundless Power, that drew
On Albion's Head the Curse to Tyrants due.
But thou appeas'd submit to Heaven's decree,
That bids this Realm of Freedom rival thee!
Now sheathe the Sword that bade the Brave att
With guiltless Blood for Madness not their ow
Sent from th' Enjoyment of their native Sho
Ill-fated- never to behold her more!
From every Kingdom on Europa's Coast
Throng'd various Troops, their Glory, Stren
With heart-felt pity fair Hibernia saw
Columbia menac'd by the Tyrant's Law:
On hostile Fields fraternal Arms engage,
And mutual Deaths, all dealt with mutual R
The Muse's Ear hears mother Earth deplore
Her ample Surface smoake with kindred Gore
The hostile Field destroys the social Ties,
And every-lasting Slumber seals their Eyes.

▲ Part of "Liberty and Peace"
by Phillis Wheatley

# Glossary

**captives**—prisoners; people held against their will

**countess**—a rank given to upperclass women in England

**dedication**—a part at the beginning of a book that names someone who is special
to the author

**illegal**—against the law

**independence**—freedom from others

**ministers**—leaders of the church

**patriotism**—love for one's country

**Patriots**—people who believed the colonies should be free from England

**plantations**—large farms that have one big crop

**protest**—to fight against something

**slave**—someone who was owned by another person and had no personal rights

**slave merchant**—an owner of one of the ships that brought slaves to the colonies

**slave trader**—a person who bought and sold slaves

**will**—a document that describes where someone's money and property go after they die